A Leaf Called Socrates

Also By Ann Holmes
Shards, Mashiko Poetry
Turn of River Press
2004

A Leaf Called Socrates
Poetry Memoir

by Ann Holmes

*To Selma and Hal,
With my love,
Ann*

iUniverse, Inc.
Bloomington

A Leaf Called Socrates
Poetry Memoir by Ann Holmes

Copyright © 2011 by Ann Holmes

All rights reserved. No part of this book may be used or reproduced by any means, graphic, electronic, or mechanical, including photocopying, recording, taping or by any information storage retrieval system without the written permission of the publisher except in the case of brief quotations embodied in critical articles and reviews.

iUniverse books may be ordered through booksellers or by contacting:

iUniverse
1663 Liberty Drive
Bloomington, IN 47403
www.iuniverse.com
1-800-Authors (1-800-288-4677)

Because of the dynamic nature of the Internet, any web addresses or links contained in this book may have changed since publication and may no longer be valid. The views expressed in this work are solely those of the author and do not necessarily reflect the views of the publisher, and the publisher hereby disclaims any responsibility for them.

Any people depicted in stock imagery provided by Thinkstock are models, and such images are being used for illustrative purposes only.

Certain stock imagery © Thinkstock.

ISBN: 978-1-4502-8144-7 (sc)
ISBN: 978-1-4502-8145-4 (ebk)

Printed in the United States of America

iUniverse rev. date: 04/18/2011

In Memory
of
Gita Peshko
Marion Hubbell
& Pete Stout

...There would still remain the never-resting mind,
So that one would want to escape, come back
To what had been so long composed....
                           Wallace Stevens

Acknowledgments

In grateful acknowledgment to the following publications for poems published or forthcoming, in the same or slightly different form: *The Connecticut Poetry Society, Connecticut River Review, Japanophile, Mediphors, Mobius,* and *Smartish Pace.*

Published poems appearing in "A Leaf Called Socrates"
  "Artichoke," *Mobius.*
  "Devil Wind," *Smartish Pace.*
  "Poetry Reading," (retitled from "Poetus Interruptus"),
    Connecticut River Review.
   Brodine Contest, honorable mention.
  "Do Not Sorry Me," retitled from "Stroke," *Mediphors.*
  "Thin King," *Mobius.*
  "Surrounded By Unfinished Women," *Long River Review, CT*
    Poetry Society.
  "Tokyo, 1945," *Connecticut River Review, Brodine Contest,*
    honorable mention.
  "Traveling Glass," *Japanophile.*

Thanks to
Billy Collins, Joan Larkin, Tom Lux, and Jean Valentine of the Sarah Lawrence College MFA faculty and Janet Flanders for her poetry workshops at The Sarah Lawrence Center for Continuing Education.

Carol Dannhauser, for her memoir workshops.
Joanna Ecke, for her poetry seminars.
Mark Shenker, for his poetry and literature seminars.

Cover Artist, Thomas S. Bernsten, photographer, gelatin silver print from "Dancing Leaves."
Copy Editor, Jacqueline Steiner.

Poets and friends, Lou Barrett, Donna Disch, Peggy Heinrich, Zdena Heller, Janet Krauss, Elsa Nad, Dick Rauh, Dale Shaw, Jacqueline Steiner, and William Ziegler; Bruni Barber, Sylvia Clark, Karolen Hodgson, Cynthia Luden, and Marilee Milroy.

Members of memoir, writing and poetry-reading workshops.

Family: sister, Jane Mason, who asks, *did that happen?;* my daughter Megan Holmes, for reading countless revisions; my husband, Jack, for his endurance; my son, Kip Holmes, and granddaughter, Lia Minonne, for their welcome distractions.

Table of Contents

When I Knew / 1
Life Span / 2
Hobo / 3
Calligraphy of Trees / 4
Chicago / 5
Dead Dog / 6
Swiss Army Knife / 7
Ludine / 8
One Winter Afternoon / 9
Live-In Grandmother / 10
Tag Sale Cameo / 11
First / 12
Last Night / 13
Timelines / 14
Letter, November, 1932 / 15
World War I Snapshots / 16
World War II in Our Sun Parlor / 17
News of the Week, 1943 / 18
Chinese Take Out / 19
When I Knew, 1944 / 21
Because / 22
Tokyo, 1945 / 23
White Cloud / 24
If Only / 26

Self Seeker / 27
My Glass / 28
Forty-Five-Minute Hour / 29
Dear Creative Soul / 30
Artichokes / 31
Surrounded by Unfinished Women / 32
Firing My Muse / 33
First Love / 34
Fogged In at Gay Head / 35
The Garden Vanishes / 36
Hawk / 37
Self Seeker / 38
Before Artists Took Over MoCa / 39

Will Venus Rise? / 40
Chinese Scroll / 41

Night Flight / 43
Roadside Shrine / 44
Peloponnese / 45
Trouble Describing Mountains / 46
Cumae Sibyl / 47
Delphi Still Life / 48
I Was Never Promised a Rose Garden / 49
Revetment / 50
Sepia Ancestors / 51
Medusa / 53
Traveling Glass / 55
Heathrow Express / 56
Night Flight / 57
Ship of Fools / 58
Packing for a Trip / 59

Hundred Geese / 61
Do Not Sorry Me / 62
Hundred Geese / 63
Key to Time / 64
Poetry Bones / 65
The Way / 66
Poetry Reading / 67
Chicago Devil Wind / 68
Thin King / 69
Roy Going Out Of His Mind / 70
Le Déjeuner sur L'Herbe / 71
Painting the Truth of Lies / 72

A Leaf Called Socrates / 73
Century Plant / 74
A Leaf Called Socrates / 75
Spring Beginning / 76
Wrapped in Leaves / 77
Irreconcilable Differences / 78
Leaving San Cresci / 79
Notes / 80

When I Knew

Life Span

They inch across bark
    creep branch
    to branch

The first I saw lay
    stretched between
    two squares

of sidewalk
    half gray fluff
    half yellow slime

squashed by a shoe
    (not mine
    I'd have died)

Their cocoons
    looked like filthy
    wads of cotton candy

Inside spun spit
    did they dream
    they'd be Monarchs?

Unfolding those
    drab wings
    they flapped

smack into
    a light bulb
    pssssssssssst

Hobo

Soon after the milkman rattled
bottles on the back porch came
a tap on the window pane
Gram opened the kitchen door
The hobo smelled of rain and cigarettes
'Scuse me Ma'am, could you spare a cup of coffee?
She sat him in the chair across from mine
Coffee perked on the gas burner
Reaching into his coat pocket
he took out a dented aluminum cup
for her to fill. She sliced him a square
of lebkuchen, hot out of the oven, baked
for her afternoon canasta game
She was too deaf to hear, *Bless you ma'am*

Calligraphy of Trees

Leaping bed to bed
arms winged for flight
I practice my journey
to the trees

Branches beckon
maple, elm
inked onto
a parchment sky

Twigs and leaves
made beasts of men
and men of beasts
and ghosts
of children asking why

The night
I take off
from the top-
most stair
      I tumble
           down
                the flight

Chicago

I used to roller skate
all over Hyde Park
& listen to the texture
of different squares of pavement
smooth cement hummed
& pebbled cement rumbled
Sometimes after a sunset
blue-gray clouds bunched
at the horizon & I'd make believe
they were mountains
until night swept the sky
& Chicago windows blazed
a geometry of light

Dead Dog

Here's this big black dog, dead
in the middle of the sidewalk
as if she decided there and then
this was mighty fine place
for a dog like her to die
I touched her eyes. *Eeuuueh*
shrieked my sister Jane—*I'm telling*
Later, sprawled on the sun parlor floor
I read, "Snip, Snap and Snur"
shaping each word with my lips
but definitely not out loud
Father snoozed in his leather chair
On radio The Andrews Sisters crooned
'don't sit under the apple tree
with anyone else but me ' In burst Jane
Whispered you-know-what into Father's ear
Behind horned rimmed glasses
his eyes swam like dirty goldfish. *Why?*
he asked. *Because live dogs won't let me*

Swiss Army Knife

The day before my seventh birthday
I ran next door to play with my friend
She's in her room, her brother said
I stepped inside. He slammed the door
Knocked me down. Sat on my stomach
Held the big blade of his Swiss Army knife
over my throat. Snapped it shut
Mother opened the door to me crying
Are you hurt? she asked. We sat
on the love seat that prickled
the backs of my legs. With her thumb
she wiped the wet off my cheeks

Ludine

shakes her rolling pin at me
Get—got no time for you

Sometimes if I beg
hard & she's in the mood

she unties her apron
unbuttons her shirt

lets me look at
her lily stab wound

lets me stroke
its jagged petals

One Winter Afternoon

on my way home from school
I walked to The Point at Lake Michigan
to watch waves splash
ice glazed granite blocks
A man grabbed my hand
Mind if I walk with you?
He yelled after me
I only meant to kiss you a little
My boots broke through snow & ice
I stopped running once I reached
the measured sidewalks
of Fifty-Fifth Street

Live-In Grandmother

Hers was the maid's room off the kitchen
She moved in years before I was born
With a sterling thimble and any old needle

she was quick to darn a sock
lower a hem, stitch together
fabric ends to quilt our beds

She believed reading ruined your eyes
and if you knocked over the salt shaker
you'd meet a stranger or kiss a fool

Each month her bird-legged friends
climbed up our six flights
of flower-carpeted stairs to play canasta

When struck down
with flu, she assumed it was I
who left death's door ajar

When I was ten
we didn't speak for two weeks
I left a note in the pantry

These have been
the happiest
two weeks in my life

Tag Sale Cameo

"Nothing is truly mine except my name"
Stanley Kunitz

Rummaging through
a Ferragamo shoe box
of junk jewelry

I found a cameo
a classic profile
of a girl with a ponytail

like those pinned
onto a board outside
tourist shops in Sorrento

I paid a dollar
to a woman
in shorts and halter

for a tag sale cameo—a far cry
from the Pre-Raphaelite
coral Gram gave my sister Jane

stolen by two burglars
the neighbors thought had come
to mow the lawn

They watched two men
empty yellow-flowered pillow slips
full of brick-a-brac

into a pick-up truck
Where were
the mower & rakes?

First

In memory of Martin Lambert, 1935-1950

At fifteen you were the first
      to be loved back
      to have sex in your eyes

That morning you were the first
      to dive off the No
      Swimming rock

We scanned the waves
      for your blond "seal" head
      First we thought it a joke

Any minute you'd splash
      out of the water
      taunt: fooled you

Days later all that was left
      of your fifteen years
      washed up on shore

Last Night

Father's left foot twitches
as mine does on the brink of sleep

He kicks off the hospital blanket
I avert my eyes from the pubic blur

Did you go dancing last night?
he asks Mother

Come closer Dear
gotta whisper

Please don't interfere
with my destiny

For once
in my life

do what I
want…

die with me

Timelines

If she'd had a mother to listen to
Eve might not have plucked
The Apple from The Tree
& palmed it off on Adam

If Salome's mother had said
don't you dare do that belly dance
The Baptist might have kept his head

The Sunday after my mother died
I all but had to sit on my hands
not to pick up the phone
& call her back

For only she
could put a stop to
whatever madness I might do

Letter, November, 1932

The rabbi dips the gold nib of his Waterman
into a bottle of blue black ink. Lifts the flange
waits for the gurgling to stop
wipes up drips with a cloth

Opens a box of Crane's stationery, eggshell white, linen weave
sent by his daughter—not yet my mother. With the pen
ordinarily reserved for the Saturday sermon
he writes his son-in-law

"if you could see fit to lend me seven hundred dollars…."

Wet words reverse on the blotter like sacred script
The envelope knifes his tongue—only a paper cut
He smiles seeing the letter sealed in blood
A week later he receives the reply

"Surely someone in your congregation…."

His son-in-law calculates fear
clear as numbers on a page—fear
he will lose his job—fear
he will stand in a breadline

The rabbi crumples the letter
tosses it into the Steuben ashtray
strikes a match. Empties charred ash
into the waste paper basket

Opens the drawer
removes the gun
frees the safety catch
tilts back his chair

World War I Snapshots

Here's my flapper Mother
knitting a soldier a sock

Fort Riley boys pose in high peak hats
knee socks and knickers

What a joke Uncle Sam played on her beaus
Fred and Eddy dead at the Argonne

Max missing in action at Belleau Wood
Bill fatally wounded at St. Mihiel

No time for Fred/Eddy/Max or Bill
to marry Mother

World War II in Our Sun Parlor

Mother loved mean-looking plants
Sharp tongue sansevieria
lined our window sills
The tabletop Emerson shaped
like a cathedral window
was only a knob turn
away from Father smoking a cigar

Every hour on the hour
ear flush against the speaker
Father shushed us

Gabriel Heatter
H.V. Kaltenborn
radio's secular priests
kept him informed

He heard words
I heard bullets, bombs, shouts
foreign correspondents
holding walkie talkies so close
they hissed their s'es

Between newscasts Father dozed
The top ten tunes played on the radio
Sometimes an ash skipped down his tie
in one perfect piece

News of the Week, 1943

I chew strands of licorice
and multi-colored jujubes
The Saturday Matinee
smells of popcorn

Handheld cameras bring war
into focus. Helmets sprout
branches. Soldiers dodge
a sideward rain of bullets

A fighter plane spirals
to the ground
P-47?
Messerschmitt?

Dinosaur tanks split
boulders. Uproot trees
A hand grenade whistles
A tank with the swastika explodes

We kids stamp and yell

Chinese Take Out

1.
Black dabs on Lee's shop window
spell "Good Luck"
Only Asians can read

At recess Jane Lee and I hang upside down
on the jungle gym. *Why good luck?* I ask
It's fortune cookie luck, Jane replies

Father and I go for Chinese take out
Our order never varies: egg rolls
egg foo young and chop suey

Jane Lee sits at a table chopping green beans
Away from blackboard walls
we're too shy to say hi

Mother empties paper cartons into china bowls
Soy sauce splatters the damask tablecloth
At last Father reads our fortunes

Everything is hard until it's easy
Many a false step is made by standing still
Do not mistake temptation for opportunity

Ridiculous, Father mutters
I bet Mr. Lee
makes them up himself

2.
The morning after
the bombing of Pearl Harbor
second grade boys
dive bomb each other

You're dead
Am not
Yes you are

We girls run to Jane
She stands alone
by the jungle gym

A girl shoves me forward
You know her best
Say it's okay

When I Knew, 1944

She sat in his chair stained
with Brilliantine
from the back of his head
He sat on the couch & lit a cigar

She had a German accent
He was good at accents
The second she left he'd do hers
A ladder ran up her lisle stocking

She picked at
the weave of her skirt
Looking at me, she said
they are killing children

He stood & sighed
Went to the front hall
for her coat. *Thank God*
we have no one there

Because

Because I didn't wear a yellow star
was not forced to go into hiding
or crammed into a freight car
I vowed to make my life matter

Did you ever try
to count your years
by the wars
you lived through?

Each suicide bomb
is a shooting star
doomed to disappear
like yesterday's headline

Last week Debby's son
called from Afghanistan
Tell me…she began
Mom, you don't want to know

Tokyo, 1945
for Nora Zecha

She leans against her mother
Her mother's hands cover her ears
The siren sounds all clear
They breathe in burning buildings

From the street their house looks the same
Inside they find an unexploded firebomb
wedged into the dining room floor
gunmetal gray
stenciled on the side

Made in the USA

The bomb pierced the roof
three ceilings, three floors
Seven round holes
as if the moon
had dropped out of the sky

White Cloud

1.
Miss Fujii bows. Sorry I'm late
I look at my watch. She's on time
We are spending the day
at the pottery village, Bizen

She points to a forest. *Fuel for firing*
comes from these red pine
In the valley below kilns climb uphill
like segmented caterpillars

A woman in a white mamasan apron drags
a wooden plank through black mud clay
A potter walks by, a board of just thrown cups
on his shoulder

Miss Fujii picks up a broken vase
half buried in the ground
blue-gray rust and orange
encrusted with ash

Bizen kilns are fired once a year
After nine days oxygen is shut off
the clay body infused
with ash and smoke

2.
We sit on the steps
of my Okayama inn
sipping sake from Bizen cups

Where are you from?
A village on the outskirts
of Hiroshima

Were you...
There?
I was there

Her hands form
an explosion
only she can see

The White Cloud
Beautiful...you can't imagine
how beautiful

Everyone came outside to see
We had no idea
what it was

Next morning THEY came
Naked   Burnt   Bald
Water, they cried

We gave water
to those who
could swallow

If Only

Eve didn't pick the apple from the tree
Oedipus took a detour at the crossroad
Helen was not so stunningly beautiful
Hamlet's father's ghost didn't come back
Cordelia was an only child
Othello didn't believe Iago
Macbeth didn't become Thane of Cawdor
Caravaggio won that tennis game
The Vienna Art Academy accepted Hitler
Sylvia's stove was electric
Lee Harvey Oswald missed
Martin Luther King skipped Memphis
The FBI listened before 9/11
Saddam Hussein asked, what WMDs?
Partly punched Miami chads counted
FEMA prepared for Katrina
I could sleep the whole night through

Self Seeker

My Glass

First line from Shakespeare's " Sonnet 22"

My glass shall not persuade me I am old
Though etched on my forehead
A cartography of roads unfold
If Robert Frost were not dead
He'd take fourteen lines to walk
The furrows of my brow
To those unmindful of the clock
Oblivious to the here and now
Who seek the road most pass by
Knowing each will lead away
When my life options fade, I
Won't mind where I stray
As my words graze this page
My glass persuades me I'm of age

Forty-Five-Minute Hour

She studies zigzag
        patterns woven
        in the Kilim

What if she swiped
        the white beach stone
        off the window sill?

Two chairs face one another
        His, Danish modern
        with matching ottoman

Hers, a La-Z-Boy
        The footrest shoots out
        when kicked just so

If she were more Buddhist
        she'd not lust
        after the milky quartz

tossed by tides
        abraded
        by the sand

She can almost feel it
        in her palm
        slippery as a lie

Dear Creative Soul

If you saw the muse poems that flood
our mailbox each month
you'd understand
our aversion to them
Yours, at least, are among the best

I like these poems
Just don't have the space
right now

I appreciate the **original story**
and **vivid imagery** but

Thank you for submitting
such strong work
however

"White Cloud"
made it into our group
of 20 semi-finalists

"Wrapped in Leaves"
came closest

We receive a great deal
of excellent material that
doesn't find its way
into the final selection

Your poems are
a little too
I don't know

Artichokes

Yes, I heard the timer ding
but I was tweaking words

I break away from my wordscape
& take the artichokes off the stove

Back inside my poem I flip
background to foreground

tip the point of view
from "me" to "you"

With chiaroscuro light and dark
I disguise hazy sfumato thoughts

Scrape out the thistle
& eat its heart

Surrounded by Unfinished Women

I model a terra cotta muse
or does she model me?
She refuses to solidify
      Elusive, she
        slips away

I punch and gouge the clay
add and take away
The muse plays hide and seek
      Reclusive, she
        slips away

I pound a heart
put it inside her breast
massage it until the beat is mine
      Intrusive, I
        slip away

Firing My Muse

My Muse is beautiful. Who would've
thought her Catherine Deneuve
with worry wrinkles that drip dry
and a benevolent evil eye

Her lizard heels pinch my feet
She's always in the judgment seat
saying, *simplify, clarify*
Her juicy syntax drains me dry

Her thoughts are mine—mine hers
The boundary between us blurs
My anima and her animus
spiral a caduceus

But who wants a two-headed snake?
Time for us to make the break
shed our skins—divorce
but would I feel remorse?

write badly
gladly or sadly?
Back off Bitch
Bitch! Bitch! echoes

her doggerel prose
Which of us is which?
Stay out of my context
my Velcro subtext

You ought to be seen
You deserve a bigger screen
I flatter her ego
& take away her say-so

First Love
from "Amor Victorious" by Caravaggio, 1602

I was eleven. Love was an angel
just my age, flesh silk
penis smiling like his lips
Feathers prickled his thigh
Scattered by Love's feet
were laurel leaves
a mandolin
a violin and bow
musical scores
a nail from The Cross
symbols unknown to me when
I gazed on Love
with the craving that grafts
a woman onto a girl

Fogged in at Gay Head

Gay Head, Martha's Vineyard

We follow less than perfect bodies
up the cliff. Wait our turn. Slip nude
into a pool of bubbling clay
I slather you with liquid earth
Easy as icing a cake

Camouflaged as
George Segal statues
we race to the ocean
rinse the glaze of anonymity
off our shivering bodies

The Garden Vanishes

        She d r i n k s
         m o r n i n g
       dew from
      his thigh
     Leaves
    rustle
   T he
  S e r
 pent
glides
branch
 to branch
  r o u n d
   that tree
    Its forked
      t o n g u e
       fl i c k s
     a parody
     of love
     T h e
   Apple
  shines
 round
 & red
& ripe
Falls in
to h e r
  h a n d
    He bites
     its glossy
      s k i n
       t a r t
     but not
     unsweet
    His lips
   graz e her
breast.The
Garden
vanish-
es

Hawk

I paint Adam and Eve
in The Garden. Casals plays
Bach Suites on CD

The phone rings. It's my daughter
from Italy. *I've moved out
no time to talk*

I look out the window
no longer confident of earth
beneath the ice-encrusted snow

A hawk lands on a branch
except for the glass
close enough to touch

Amber eyes blink back
my startled gaze
Brown feathers

ruffle and align
Wings fold as if
posing for Brancusi

Adam and Eve fidget
on the easel. Casals hums
louder than his cello

My daughter hangs up
The hawk takes off
I glaze a Bosch bubble

over Adam and Eve
so they may stay
in The Garden

Self Seeker

Like a mockingbird, I fugue
medleys from others

pastiche images from Old Masters
borrow Narcissus from Boltraffio

paint him in a weeping cave
scarf him in Titian crimson

His pond becomes my stream

Where is my reflection?
Where is my reflection?

Before Artists Took Over MoCA
*Museum of Contemporary Art,
North Adams, MA*

Ed shows me the half moon
burnt into the floorboard
where Mama sat rolling capacitors
in Building Four of Sprague Electric
She had to stuff cotton her ears
not to hear the grinding and grating

Before MoCA opened, curators
gave guards a crash course
in modern art. Some visitors tell Ed
they like hearing what he has to say
better than listening to the MoCA guides

This morning I hear the footsteps
of a few visitors in the room upstairs
looking at The Seasons by Anselm Kiefer
Building Four is quiet, except
for its creaking floorboards

Will Venus Rise?

A Delft vase swings from a rope
Botticelli grabs it. The Delft
becomes a piñata
I whack at with a #12 brush
Blue & white shards
shatter by my feet. Out fall
two Daumier magistrates
Like *The Cat in the Hat*
they bow & doff their top hats
The one wearing spectacles
hands me the Mary half
of a Fra Angelico annunciation
Not an angel in sight
Mary, Mary, so contrary
I skateboard back to my easel
Ideas arrive in installments
I'm on sabbatical from content
but where's Venus?

Chinese Scroll

Evening mist blurs
brush strokes
on twisted pine
I nearly miss
the inch high
naked monk
bent over
the steep
mountain path
scarcely care
whether
he reaches
the tea hut
perched
on the rock
so precipitously

Night Flight

Roadside Shrine
Taygetos mountains, Sparta, Greece

Birds too far away
to identify
bound for some bird task
Where will thy alight?

A shrine on stilts
marks where
a wingless car
flew off the road

I unlatch
the glass door
to a Byzantine saint
torn from a book

A wick floats
in a jam-jar
of olive oil
I light the flame

Peloponnese

Color coded
bee boxes
strung over
the hillside
each with
a queen bee

a laundry line
of rainbow skirts
single-pole tents
pickup trucks
parked every
which way

A donkey pulls
an empty cart
followed by
a farmer
two sheep
and a goat

Does the man
on the porch
of the small
whitewashed
church know
he's too tall
to fit inside

Trouble Describing Mountains

You know how a cloud squats
on a mountain top
fluffs a pillow
of sunlit rock
as if to bed down
with a good book

I'd like to skip stones
over waves
& waves
of mountains

If I were a mountain goat
I'd blend right into
these no-color rocks
You'd never see hide
nor hair of me

Cumae Sibyl

The cave air chills my arms
Christina, our guide, identifies
where the Cumae sibyl fasted

chewed on laurel leaves
shouted oracles, even telling of
the birth of Christ

Outside, wild dogs dart
from a patch of shade
to a patch of sun

Christina fingers
her sun-streaked hair
directs our gaze

to the temple of Jupiter
converted to
a Christian basilica

now a pile of rubble
that the Cumae dogs
squat over

Delphi Still Life

On the way to Delphi
our guide points out the crossroad
where Oedipus killed his father
as if it happened

Weeds sprout out of the sybil rock
fallen from the Phaedriades
I stand where she stood
predicting the Trojan War

The theater is roped off after
two thousand years of feet
We can't skip tier to tier
pretend to hear
Aeschylus & Sophocles

Here's the mountain Aesop
climbed, enemies at his heels
Despite the clever fox he was
they pushed him off the cliff

On marble *metope*
along The Sacred Way
a goddess rides sidesaddle
with half a head, half a smile

A headless god spears
a skirted goddess, limbs askew
as if bodies were walls
to break through

I Was Never Promised a Rose Garden

Our Ekali house was on Mount Pendeli
an hour north of Athens, where marble
was quarried to build the Parthenon
Each night from our balcony we'd see
the casino lights of Mt. Parnitha
That was when we had our very own
rose garden with paths & trellises
& a gardener, stick-thin Old Nicolaides
who came with the house
When I failed to see Old Nicolaides
puttering over a desiccated rose
or dusting with his toxic powder
I feared he'd been struck comatose
jabbed by a thorn of a blood-red rose

Revetment

A three-legged tourist, fresh
from the riddle of the sphinx

clacks up the marble staircase
of the Athens Byzantine Museum

I follow the tkk-tkk-tkk of his walking stick
into a roomful of icons sheathed in silver

holes cut out for the heads and hands
What are these? the tourist asks

Revetment, I reply—a name
I read off a museum label

Icons of Mary, Jesus and the saints
The Greeks touch & kiss them when they pray

Silver protects the paintings
from dirty hands & moist lips

Bet you five Euros, nothing's underneath
Why paint what you don't see?

Outside the Athens wind whips
strands of silver across my eyes

Sepia Ancestors

Garbage day in Erythrea
Blue plastic bags line the curbs
A sepia photograph of Yaya
and her six mustached sons
leans on a yellow basket
frame askew
                glass cracked

When Yaya gave birth
to son after son
behind the curtained door
did she forget to hang
the blue-eyed charm
to deceive
                the evil eye?

Six dressed in Sunday best
Hair trimmed
Handkerchiefs poke
out of coat pockets
Mud from artichoke fields
clings to shoes scuffed
                past polishing

Yaya's hands that scrub and sweep
rest on her apron. Black skirt
bunches over the carpet
When did she have time
to embroider a garland
of six-petal flowers
                    on her shawl?

I load Yaya, her six sons
and the yellow basket
into my hatchback
Before today I doubt
a son strayed more than
a donkey ride
                    from home

Medusa

after Edward Burne-Jones' "Perseus Series"

Asleep on my granite bed, I dream
    I turn the whole world to stone
    Wake with a smile

Comb my snakes into a crown
    Perseus sees me reflected
    in Athena's shield

I can't see him
    cloaked in his invisibility
    With his diamond sword

he lops off my head
    Throws it into a bag
    fastens winged slippers

to his heels. We soar over
    a sea I can't see
    Ionian? Aegean?

Perseus swoops down to rescue
    Andromeda, chained
    to a rock, about to be devoured

by a ravenous serpent
    (though most I know
    are vegetarian)

He slays the serpent, frees
    Andromeda, flees
      to an island west of east

Cycladic? Dodecanese?
    My head rolls onto the grass
    Trees and a well are all I see

Perseus lifts up my head
    My reflection floats
    on the well water

I flash him a beguiling smile
    splash him with
    my rhinestone tears

Look at Medusa
    he tells Andromeda
    She looks

He kisses lips
    she can't lift in a smile
    I turn her heart to alabaster

Traveling Glass

On the train
to Yokohama

traveling glass
spreads my

cheek bones
slants my eyes

strips me of my
western mask

Heathrow Express

Across the aisle
two young women
read paperbacks
Rotten Times
& *Dreams Come True*

Rotten Times
licks her unlipsticked lips
Combat boots
jiggle to the wheel
clickety clack

Dreams Come True's
pashmina shawl
dips & folds
as if primed
to do just that

HEATHROW: END OF THE LINE

Rotten Times
tosses her who-done-it
on the seat. Heaves
her khaki colored rucksack
to her shoulders

Dreams Come True
marks her place
with a tasseled bookmark
Slips her gothic romance
into a side pocket
of her Louis Vuitton valise

Night Flight

Wing light blinks red
Dawn drags

the drowsy sky
from the ocean bed

I want you to see the tops of clouds
Gram told my child self

A Pakistani swathed in orange
palms her way down the aisle

Sleepers wake
to coffee brewing

Ship of Fools
in memory of Pete Stout

You stumble into my dream
from wherever the dead live
Is it too late? I ask. *Too late,* you echo
Death dims each attachment to life
When you learned you had lung cancer
you invited me on an Alaskan cruise
Three days out of San Francisco
I felt I was about to die. I sipped chamomile
The sommelier filled your flute with Brut
At Glacier Bay we watched humpbacks breach
& slap the water with their broad flat tails
Heard the muted thunder of glaciers calve
& splinter into nothingness
Now my deaf eyes can't see
the negative space you inhabit
On your way out of my dream
you ask, *do I know you?*

Packing for a Trip

is like preparing for death
yet for death there's no need to fret
over what to take

Thirty thousand feet above the Atlantic
I worry about that carton of milk
souring in the refrigerator

The dead grieve over
words unsaid
the loss of tomorrow

I see the dead queued
before a stop light sunset
waiting for life's

traffic to abate
before crossing
to the other side

Hundred Geese

Do Not Sorry Me

   do not SORRY me
      surprised to be alive
         should have died
           body okay
              not paralyzed

            night please
       do NOT ask me
     to answer questions
 at night   depressed night   I cry

If second stroke
    kill patient
       flush ashes
           down toilet

      dreamt couldn't
   push open hard books
once I was front of first
I was angry   I was left

I'm okay right?
   except symbol can't
      come out mouth
         in speech

        hopital   hopistal
          afixit   afazic
       aproxyia   aproseeyah
      can't see   these my lips

Hundred Geese

First dream
after the stroke
I wait
at a bus stop

Breaks screech
hundreds
of geese
fly by in a "V"

Last words
stamped in
red hot
authority

Sometimes
the world seems
bizarre
beyond belief

Key To Time

I lift the lid off a red leather box
shoved behind the desk drawer
Don't, warns Mother

From time to time she makes
a guest appearance in a dream
Inside I find a white jade necklace

The string snaps, beads recoil
perhaps offended by
the warmth of my hand

bounce on the floor, change
into white mice and scurry off
The key, the key, Mother cries

Wedged beneath the lid
is the burnished Key to Time
I scrape it free. Fit it

into the front hall clock
no one ever remembers to set
I try to nudge the small hand

a moment forward
a moment back
but Time will not budge

Poetry Bones

All I know is I'm leading thirty-seven
poets, vagrants, penitents
wandering fiefdom to fiefdom
searching for poetry bones
I don't know why there are
thirty-seven, not three and seven
or why I am in charge
nothing you'd catch me at awake
I don't know if these thirty-seven
with their middle age patina
took a wrong turn into my dream
where far as I know no poetry bones
are buried. In fact I don't even know
what poetry bones are
what they look like
what I'd do if I found them
call in an archeologist?
erect a shrine? throw the *I Ching*?
flesh them into a poem?

The Way

An arcane sect of monks
in night goggles
and putty-colored cloaks

moves toward me
I step aside to let them pass
as I would a herd of goats

Chants echo off polygonal walls
An elder tugs my sleeve
Come or you lose The Way

I follow nonstop fugues
across a timber bridge
over a riverbed of crazed earth

We climb sedimentary cliffs
strewn with bones left by war
famine and plague

The rosy dawn unveils
rocks toppled from
The Tower of Babel

Monks squat on stones
unlace their sandals
dust grit from their toes

An elder hands me
a putty-colored cloak
& a pair of night goggles

Poetry Reading
to Eamon Grennan

A dead swan spread upon the sand
no wound visible—no clue why she died

The poet lifts a wing. Measures the wing span
Six feet. Wing springs shut

The poet reads at a gallery
of black and white photography

Two women saunter in
pause between photographs

of a fence and barn
a nude and face. Squeeze

behind the poet. Trample
the dead swan. The poet reads on

predicts scavengers will come
His words pick her clean

I welcome these intruders
They delay her decay

Chicago Devil Wind

On the corner of Harper and Fifty-Third Street
Devil Wind whistles into her husband's ear
wait here—not a word of where she's off to
or what she will do once there

Billowing currents of air into her blue-black skirt
Devil Wind leaps to clouds, still as a picture
not doing what they ought to do—in fact
doing nothing at all

A cloud butterfly won't change
to a llama; a llama won't change
to a lion; a lion won't change
to a clown; a clown won't change
to an old man frowning

Scenting her breath with hazelnut
chamomile, rosehip hibiscus
Devil Wind howls at clouds
till vaporous elbows poke
this way and that

The higher Devil Wind flies
she spies clouds still higher
Only with a digital telescope
can you see, east of the Milky Way
the smear of her blue-black skirt

Thin King

Thinking is what the Thin King does
but in the land of Drowse & Doze
where thinking is a felony
The Thin King is sentenced to hard words
The gavel bangs. Wakes him from his reverie

From Monday through Sunday
a spider warden crochets
crossword webs
from gossamer threads
spun by silkworms in the garden

The Thin King frowns
at unheard of words
flips pages of the OED
for synonyms from A to Z

In the mean-spirited mean time
The Thin King serves time behind
candy cane bars too sweet to lick
Peppermint makes him sick

He checks out the poetry & prose
from the prison library of Drowse & Doze
On the shelves are all sorts of books
perusable by kings and crooks

There's a moral here I suppose
that even in the land of Drowse & Doze
where thinking is a crime, no one imprisons
the mind, for there's never a time
when The Thin King stops thinking

Roy Going Out of His Mind

I go to Stamford to pick up Roy
He opens the door
His once lush philodendron hasn't a leaf

The apartment was bugged
so I cut off the leaves
Bugged by what? white fly? I'd like to ask

I lift Roy's feet into the jeep
We drive to a restaurant by Long Island Sound
Later over a glass of Beaujolais Nouveau

I ask Roy what's going on
Hooded turquoise eyes
look up from massacred duck

This conversation is boring me
I resent people like you
who pretend to be interested

After dinner, I lift Roy's feet into the jeep
We watch a crimson sunset
in a teal blue sky—too lurid for a poem

Déjeuner sur L'Herbe

After Edouard Manet, "Lunch on the Grass," 1863.

We sit on grass, wet with dew
I unpeel foil off camembert
André gives me a swig of Pinot Noir
Stefan hands me a baguette

André says, *et bien, Babette,*
take off your fucking frock
I laugh—why not?
Andre unbuttons my dress

Stefan unlaces my corset
I kick off my petticoat
roll down my stockings,
unbuckle my boots

My toes knead prickly blades of grass
A gentle wind fans my unpinned hair
André & Stefan fuss about Manet
Neither got into le salon de refusé

A woman wearing a toga
beckons me over
Her toga drifts to the ground
We sit cross-legged

on sun-warmed grass
She weaves sprigs of lavender
into my hair, licks the stain
of Pinot Noir off my lips

Painting the Truth of Lies
After Max Beckmann's "The Actors," 1941-42

Beckmann was witness to a shameful age
the world his triptych, a painted stage
He painted the rage of Europe
a sideshow of actors, musicians, crooks & spies
Two-faced Janus, blind on his pedestal
A king with a feathery cloak
stabs himself in the heart
(Is his bloody dagger real or a prop?)
On the steps, off to one side
is a man who scans the headlines
of The New York Times. Beside him
are shackled ankles & bare feet
A woman with an unfocused gaze
wears a string of pearls & a pink chemise
holds up a mirror to her deadpan face
trying to remember the calm of an altarpiece

A Leaf Called Socrates

Century Plant
in memory of Ginny McFarland

The night after Ginny's memorial service
I dreamt she grabbed a spare body

off a hanger from the front hall closet
searching for someone new to wear

Anyone will do she said, waving
to those of us who could see her

Ginny's Century plant
had bloomed a few months ago

Ginny phoned everyone she knew
Come quickly—It lasts only a day

A Leaf Called Socrates
in memory of Marion Hubbell

Alfred paints Marion a rose, white
in the morning light

A petal becomes a feather
called Snow Queen

Caught between
the window & screen

is a leaf called Socrates
A sunflower grows

from a seed thrown
to the crows

A sunflower bows
to the scavengers she fed

Spring Beginning

In memory of Gita Peshko, 1934-1985

I want to show you
spring beginning
even here on city streets

Where are we by the way?
Good to locate poems
and dreams

See these trees?
I grew up with city trees
Stunted buds on knotted twigs

Here, look through my eyes
Red caterpillar flowers
splatter the sidewalks

and stain my shoes
See these cherry blossoms?
I like them weeping

I follow the cherry blossoms on your kimono
upstairs into a roomful of clouds
by The Cloud Master

Sometimes I pick up the phone
and hear your voice. It's someone else
You have no voice

Your body's
hills and valleys
winter still

Beyond your vanishing
point do you see
spring beginning?

Wrapped in Leaves
in memory of Gita Peshko

We escape when no escape seems possible
Leaves shield us. Your leaf-green sari
acts as camouflage

You lead me toward an unknown city—Katmandu?

Remember poinsettia, red as Christmas
boys climbing up to the shrine
rocks strapped to their foreheads?

Like Sisyphus, you said

Red and yellow leaves
push against the picture plane
spill out the frame

Like a Mannerist painting, you might have said

You and I gather leaves
but not as fast
as they fall

I paste them on with spit
You grab a paintbrush
chlorophyll them green

I position my hands, finger
to finger, thumb to thumb
form an Islamic arch

You step through my finger frame
Your vines entwine my knuckles
Wrapped in leaves, you leave

Irreconcilable Differences
in memory of Pete Stout

On Compo Beach a woman yells
into her cell phone to someone
not nearly as far away as you

You gave me back a piece of myself
in my letters you returned
See me pick white cat hairs

off my skirt, grade essays
on Melville's archetype
of good and evil

Those Siamese cats are long gone
Even now I gauge shades of gray
trying to undo good from evil

What I hate most
about your death
it makes me deaf to you

In the Hopper postcard
"Rooms by the Sea" I sent you
sunlight angles onto a bare wall

I anchor you in Hopper blue
Do you see me
behind death's wall

inside Hopper's furnished room?
Do you hear me praise
life's clutter?

Leaving San Cresci

Once this room stored wine and oil
maybe even goats and chickens
Now the walls are plastered with handswirls
The linen on the bed, time yellowed
Reflected in the mirror is half a marriage portrait
your landlady's ancestor or someone bought
I leave the door ajar. Thunder
stumbles over the mountains—Apennine
applause for my ten days here
Beneath sliced tree crossbeams
unglazed tiles take on the flesh tones
of Lia's baby body
The mirror mirrors no one
Whoever she is, gone to glass

Notes

1. Marion Hubbell named an autumn leaf, Socrates, trapped between her kitchen window and screen.

2. Epigraph, Wallace Stevens, "The Poems of Our Climate" *The Collected Poems*, 1965-1990, p. 193.

3. Tag Sale Cameo, p. 11. "Passing Through," Stanley Kunitz, *The Collected Poems*, pp. 238, 239, Norton, 2000.

4. If Only, p. 26. Ruth Krauss, *If Only*, p. 25, Toad Press, 1969, and her poem, "If Only" (*I'll Be You and You Be Me....*).

5. My Glass, p. 28. From Billy Collins' prompt, taking the first line of a Shakespeare sonnet for a sonnet of your own. I use imagery of Robert Frost, *The Poetry of Robert Frost*, Holt Rinehart Winston, 1969, "The Road Not Taken," p. 105.

6. Self Seeker, p. 39, Giovanni Antonio Boltraffio, (follower of Leonardo) 1466/7-1516.

7. Fogged in at Gay Head, p. 36. The clay cliffs and hot springs at Gay Head State Beach (partially, nudist) at Martha's Vineyard, Massachusetts, are now environmentally protected. Once people climbed the cliffs and dipped into hot bubbly clay, and afterwards, paraded around, looking like George Segal plaster statues.

8. Before the Artists Took Over MoCA, p. 40. Article on Joe Manning, *The Advocate*, Fairfield County CT, July 24, 2002, p. 31.

9. Cumae Sibyl, p. 47. The Cumae caves are located near Naples. The Cumae sibyl delivered the Apollonian oracle at Cumae.

10. I Was Never Promised a Rose Garden, p. 49. From 1980 to 1983, we lived in a northern suburb of Athens.

11. Sepia Ancestors, pp. 51. *Yaya* is Greek for grandmother and old woman. In 1923, the Greek and Turkish governments exchanged

populations. Greeks from Smyrna settled in Nea (new) Erytrea, north of Athens. Erytrea is in the valley below Mt. Pendeli.

12. Do Not Sorry Me, p. 62. From my hospital notes after a stroke in 1991. (This was when I first began to write poetry.)

13. Poetry Reading, p. 67. Eamon Grennan reading, 2004, at Silvermine Guild Gallery of Art, New Canaan, Connecticut, ; *So it Goes*, "Swan In Winter," p. 70, Graywolf Press, 1995.

14. Irreconcilable Differences, p. 78. From "Rooms by the Sea" by Edward Hopper, 1951, Yale University Art Gallery, New Haven, Connecticut.